TWO GLASGOW STREET PERFORMERS

by

For Bob
Best Wishes
July 2009.

Stuart McMillan

A short history of two Irish entertainers who made Glasgow their home – one an itinerant performer who made his living by juggling and conjuring whom the Glasgow people took to their hearts; the other had an accomplished dexterity with wire who made and sold chains and puzzles as a living but through drink the Glasgow people lost any respect they had for him.

Step One
of the
"Step Series"

Published by
The Smiddy Press
Glasgow

First published 2009 by
The Smiddy Press
"Steppingstones", 5A Bellevue Road, Kirkintilloch, Glasgow. G66 1AL.
Scotland

ISBN: 978-0-9563113-0-6

**An Edition limited
to 500 copies
of which this is**

No. 24

Printed and bound by
Clydeside Press Ltd.,
37 High Street, Glasgow Cross, Glasgow. G1 1LX
Scotland

PREFACE

Malabar was one of Glasgow's best loved characters of the nineteenth century who few people have now heard of. There were a number of articles reminiscing about him in newspapers and the occasional mention in a few books after his death. J. B. Findlay published a short history of Malabar in 1945 called *"JUGGLING THROUGH FOUR REIGNS"*, which is now very scarce. I have been interested in Malabar, collecting information over the years, and have managed to find new details and extra photographic information. Because of this I felt, after over 60 years since J. B. Findlay's history, it was time to publish an updated history of Malabar's life.

"Penny-a-Yard" was another Glasgow character of which very little is written – what there is I have gathered together in this book.

Stuart McMillan.

Isn't it strange that princes and kings
And clowns that caper in sawdust rings
And common folks like you and me
Are builders of eternity?

To each is given a bag of tools,
A shapeless mass and a book of rules,
And each must make, ere life has flown,
A stumbling block or a steppingstone.

R. L. Sharpe

Step - One

Acknowledgments

Any biography can only be produced with the help of others. My greatest debt of gratitude is to Gordon Bruce who has collected Malabar material for some time and has given information and advice unstintingly. His knowledge of books and showmen of the past is second to none. It was a great pity when his house was broken into a few years ago and the oil painting of Malabar was stolen. Fortunately he had a photograph of it which is reproduced on page 23, perhaps some day this painting will be returned to its rightful owner.

I am grateful to the following individuals; - Graham Hunter from the Panoptican Music Hall Trust who brought the book *Rural Rambles Round Glasgow and Queer Folk* to the attention of Gordon Bruce; Martin MacGilp who brought the newspaper cuttings book *The Dark Side of Glasgow* and the Glasgow Poor Law database both in the Mitchell Library to my attention; Peter Lane for information and a picture of Malabar I had not come across; Fiona Hayes curator of the People's Palace in Glasgow; Winnie Tyrrell of the Burrell Collection (Culture and Sport Glasgow (Museums)); the late John Turner; Adam McNaughtan; Joe Fisher and the staff at the Mitchell Library in Glasgow. I would also like to acknowledge the help of Jim Hogg at Edinburgh City Library and Sharon Scullion at the Archdiocese of Glasgow.

Apart from the above I must acknowledge the help from my friend David Barnaby and my family who have pointed out many mistakes to be corrected as well as acknowledging the help of my eldest daughter June who taught me how to use a computer and was always there to help when I needed it.

Contents

Illustrations

Malabar (1800 – 1883)

It is generally accepted that "Malabar" was born in County Sligo on 20th February, 1800. His real name was Patrick Feeney [1] the son of a small Irish farmer by the same name. Unlike his two elder brothers he was not in any way academic, he had been to school for a while but he did not learn much. His industrious brothers looked down on him, thought he was lazy and he decided to leave home and see more of the world. He had heard much of Dublin and decided to leave home to find his way there without knowing what he was going to do. His elder brothers helped him in this quest by giving him thirty shillings as a start to his travels. He travelled to Dublin and after a week looking around the city he survived by taking odd jobs but soon his savings had dwindled to his last shilling. Thinking he might find more secure employment in England he made his way down to the wharf, and found the master of a small sailing ship who allowed him to work his passage to Liverpool.

It was near Liverpool docks where his attention was drawn to a large crowd of people in the street, they were watching the performance of a Chinese juggler. Young Patrick Feeney joined the crowd and was captivated with this Oriental's performance and followed the juggler from pitch to pitch about the streets until dusk. It was so new and strange to him he could not get enough. When night came he had no money to pay for his lodging so he spent the night in an empty shed near the docks. Next day he woke hungry and cold with no money left and found the Chinese juggler performing whom he again followed. After a while he summoned up enough courage to go up and offer his services to help him carry his apparatus. To his great joy his offer was accepted. He was faint and hungry that day having eaten nothing whatever since the night before. When darkness fell the Chinese juggler took him to his lodging house giving him a good meal which put him right again.

That is how he entered the profession by becoming a servant to the old original Tusang, the Chinese Juggler [2] who came to this country before the great Indian juggler Ramo Samee. His duties with Tusang were to carry his apparatus and to clean them every morning before going out to perform. Young Patrick Feeney never cleaned the props without having a practice with them and was managing quite well until one day Tusang caught him at it. Tusang went into a rage, he didn't lay a hand on him but he cursed Patrick in his Chinese language. After a while he cooled down and wanted to see what Patrick could do. Young Patrick showed him and he seemed astonished at the young lads skill. In a few days Tusang got a Chinese costume for him and he performed with Tusang in the streets. He became his apprentice, learning the craft of juggling and acrobatics as well as performing strong-man in front of crowds of people. What he lacked in education he soon gained in skill and it was not long before young Patrick Feeney was in some things, better than his master. Tusang allowed him to address the crowd and quite often he heard people say how the young Chinese juggler had a fine Irish accent. Not only did Tusang give Patrick Feeney his skill which provided a livelihood until the end of his life, he also gave him the name "Malabar" a name he proudly bore all his days.

After a period of nearly a year, when they were at Newcastle-upon-Tyne [3] Malabar decided to leave Tusang, he shook his mentor's hand and for the first time set out on his own as an itinerant performer, travelling to Scotland. Malabar met Tusang again once or twice at fairs and such where he was performing in opposition to him. This was awkward as Tusang did not like competing with his apprentice and Malabar had a guilty conscience with having to take money away from his old master but each had to make a living. [4]

When he arrived in Scotland he appeared in Glasgow at the Glasgow Fair in 1822 or 1823 probably as an act in a circus. [5] Among the exhibitions he remembered seeing at Glasgow Fair that first time was Pollito's wild beast show, Antony Powell's Circus, Ord's Circus, Bartley Minch's Show and Kit Newsome's Circus. Also there was the Italian

Cardoni family who had just arrived in Glasgow which included Old Mr. Cardoni (who died around 1836 at the age of 102) plus his sons who were practising juggling at this time.   Old Cardoni assisted Malabar in obtaining some apparatus;   Malabar was given the opportunity to practise with them after which Old Cardoni engaged Malabar to perform.   Malabar said Old Cardoni was the first Punch and Judy show to appear in Glasgow and that he was once engaged to perform Punch and Judy before George the Third and the Royal family, that honour which he boasted of until the day he died.

Glasgow Fair was established between the years 1189-1198 when King William authorised Bishop Jocelyn to hold a fair in Glasgow for eight days.   Originally the fair included selling cattle and horses along with the hiring of servants.   Shows such as circuses, theatres, Punch & Judy, waxworks, menageries and all sorts of booths did not arrive till the early 19th century.[6]   The shows during Glasgow Fair were said to be the best in Europe. They were situated on the Green at the bottom of the Saltmarket opposite the High Court in and around the area called Jail Square until 1871 when they moved to Vinegar Hill.[7]

Ord's Circus at Glasgow Fair.

Malabar was a tall,[8] powerfully built man with strong features.   His deportment was graceful although manly and he spoke quietly yet with a blend of quiet humour.   How Tusang dressed is not known nor do we know if Malabar replicated his appearance but the peculiar costume he wore most of his life was unique, along with his name, giving him an enigmatic illusion of oriental ambiance.   He made quite an impression on the public while walking through the streets of Glasgow to one of his favourite spots.   A tall figure wearing a turban, loose brightly striped baggy pants and gaudy robe down to his knees with a leather belt tied around his waist, (the letters inscribed on it making the word MALABAR), his juggling and conjuring apparatus in a canvas bag hanging at the end of a stick carried over his shoulder.

This painting is from the People's Palace in Glasgow.   It is very similar to the picture in
'Original Coloured Drawings of Edinburgh Characters and Others' by Edmund Holt.
Edmund Holt died on 20th September 1892.

Sam Wild in his book *Old Wild's* tells us his father James Wild engaged the equilibrist Malabar for his show. He balanced coach wheels, a plank twenty-one feet long, and a live donkey on a ladder. It could have been in James Wild's show that Malabar learned conjuring.[9] In his early years his main programme consisted of turning somersaults, balancing a heavy coach-wheel on his chin, in one Glasgow Fair he balanced the coach wheel twenty-three times in one day in Phillip's Circus on the Green. He also performed Japanese top-spinning, juggling with brass balls, rings, and daggers, throwing a brass ball to a great height in the air and cleverly catching it in a metal cup strapped to his forehead, throwing a heavy steel cannon ball high in the air which he caught on the back of his neck, rolling it up and down his arms, threading a string of beads with his mouth and the amusing feat of balancing a donkey strapped to the side of a ladder. David Prince Miller in his book *The Life Of A Showman* notes, *"When opposite Astley's Amphitheatre, a large crowd attracted my attention, they were witnessing the performance of a very clever boy, one of a company of show people, he was tossing in the air knives, rings, balls etc., and catching them in a very dexterous manner; after a part of the performance had been exhibited, a collection was made among the spectators; the hat was held to me, I certainly was very much pleased with the performance, and gave the man a shilling, prompted as much by desire to show off as to be liberal, for in the act of dropping the shilling into the hat, I did not forget to call out loud enough to be heard, and with great pomp, "Here, my man, is a shilling for you;" notwithstanding this, the man, after he had pretended to count the money, said in his harangue to the assembled crowd, "he had been round among all this 'ere lot of people and all the money he'd got was seven pence halfpenny! - there is just seven of us, and the donkey; so that it's only a penny a piece, and a halfpenny for the donkey; and I cannot think of allowing the exhibition to go unless we get eighteen pence, vich I considers is little enough for our trouble, so if you makes up ten pence halfpenny more among you, you shall see the whole performance, and the strong man will balance the donkey on his chin." In a very few seconds lots of coppers were showered into the ring –I should think at least three shillings' worth- but the showman was not an adept at calculation, and upon counting the cash, he said, "It was all right excepting three half pence- three half pence more and up goes the donkey!" Another shower of coppers- I may venture to say to the value of a shilling, the rest of the performance took place, and up went the donkey."[10]* Now it would be foolish of me to say this was definitely Malabar he saw perform.[11]

Malabar said he was the first to balance the donkey in this country and he was commanded by George the Fourth to perform it at Ascot. He explained how he performed it…

> The donkey was a little one (his last one was called Bob) and was only about eight and a half stones in weight. When he called Bob he would come trotting up to the ladder like a dog. Malabar prepared this trick by putting the donkey's fore-legs over the top spoke of a ten foot ladder which was wider than a normal ladder. Then the donkey's hind legs went between the next spoke and the one below that again so that he was sitting on the third spoke from the top. He then fixed the head strap round its neck which kept its head fast to the top of the ladder. He needed someone to help him raise the donkey and ladder to his chin. Malabar ensured he did not keep the donkey up too long. When Bob grew too heavy he sold him.

Some people had heard Malabar balanced a lad with a wooden leg whilst the lad played the fiddle. It appears David Prince Miller told this story but Malabar said it was not him but that it was Nicolson who performed this who was a very strong man, even stronger than himself.[12]

© Peter Lane

Old Malabar drawing from Peter Lane's collection.

'Lord' George Sanger, in his book *Seventy Years a Showman*, tells of the time he was with his father's peep show at the great Hyde Park Fair. Malabar was at the fair performing by juggling with knives, bottles and balls, bringing out a donkey strapped to the side of a sixteen rung ladder, putting a tin plate in the centre of the small arena, and saying, *"If you wish to see the remaining and most remarkable part of the exhibition, I leave it to your generosity to contribute a little more. There is the plate, ladies and gentlemen; don't be afraid of throwing in your money, I shall not be afraid of picking it up!"* In response, coppers would be sure to come rolling in. Then, looking at the plate, Malabar would say: *"Ah, I see there is so much. If you make it up to level money, up goes the donkey. Tuppence more, ladies and gentlemen; only tuppence more, and up goes the donkey!"* The coppers would be forthcoming and Malabar would lift the ladder and balance the donkey in the air. Then the show was cleared for another audience. He goes on to say how Malabar's donkey was stolen the second day of the fair. Having searched for the animal in vain it was arranged that young George Sanger would take the place of the donkey so the show could go on. He did the trick and was duly balanced in mid air climbing to the top of the sixteen rung ladder, supported on the chin, forehead, shoulder and arm of the juggler. At the time Malabar would be twenty seven years older than the young George Sanger. This was his main trick in his early to middle years but as time went on and he got older, the donkey disappeared and his speciality was catching the ball in the cup strapped to his forehead. He used the same "patter" only it became, *"tuppence more, ladies and gentlemen; only tuppence more, and up goes the ball,"* instead of up goes the donkey.

He was a strong young man when he came to Glasgow in his early twenties. In addition to balancing a donkey on the ladder he threw a heavy cannonball in the air and caught it on the back of his neck. When Bob, Malabar's last patient four legged companion was sold, he placed a big boy on the ladder and as he elevated him the humorist quaintly said: *"I'll give this boy a rise in the world."*

William Dinsmore in his article "Old Malabar, Juggler and Acrobat," notes that Malabar said he originated the well known phrase *"Tuppence more, ladies and gentlemen, and up goes the donkey."* The phrase he said was adopted by Edwin Waugh as a heading to chapter two of his 1881 book *Besom Ben Stories*.

Many people think the phrase *"Tuppence more and up goes the donkey"* was a phrase used by showmen at fairs to obtain more money and the trick was never performed. There are numerous accounts of this trick being performed. Brenda Assael in her book *Circus and Victorian Society* on page sixty-six says, *"One penny showman told the Morning Chronicle in 1850 that formerly he had strapped a donkey to a ladder and balanced him. But the papers attacked the performance and I was taken to the Union Hall ... and fined 7s 6d and they kept the donkey in default, referring to the anticruelty law of 1849 protecting domestic animals."* On July 3rd 1881 *The New York Times* published an article from *The London Field* which said, *"I was irresistibly reminded of a performance I used some years ago to see in the streets of London, when a group of itinerant acrobats used to tie a small donkey to the top rungs of a ladder, raise it to the perpendicular position, and wait for a contribution of coppers sufficient to induce him to balance the ladder with the donkey on top, on the chin of the strongman of the party, the shower of coins being stimulated by the exclamation of "Tuppence more, and up goes the donkey."* [13]

Malabar could be seen at Glasgow Green during the Glasgow Fair or at New Year times, when shows of every conceivable description centred on Glasgow Green. He would get an engagement from some of the managers and would appear on the outside stage where his tall commanding figure dressed in gaudy robes was sure to draw a crowd. Someone would be shouting out the wonders to be seen inside while Malabar exhibited some of his popular feats to entice the people to pay for admission. [14]

Glasgow Fair in Malabar's time had an incredible amount of shows of all sizes. The noise of showmen blowing trumpets, banging drums or clanging bells to draw the public's attention to listen to their spiel of the wonders to be found inside their booth or tent added to the excitement of the crowds and locomotion through the shows was a work of infinite difficulty; David Prince Miller's booth once attracted 96,000 Glaswegians in 13 days.[15]

Imagine John Henry Anderson "The Wizard of the North" who built his ill fated City Theatre in Glasgow Green, a huge building capable of holding 5,000 people when it opened at Glasgow Fair on Saturday 12th July in 1845 only to last four months before it was burnt to the ground on the 19th of November. After he performed before Queen Victoria at Balmoral Castle he erected a fantastic Magic Temple at Glasgow Fair in 1850, whose frontage was 240 feet long and 120 feet in breadth. This was a replica of Balmoral Castle with towers, battlements and gables. Inside there were two large cone shaped marquees each capable of holding 1,500 people. In one was Mr Baylis with his ingenious automata along with the incredible Lauri family who were performing gymnasts and other entertainments; in the other Professor Anderson the wizard performed his dexterous and mysterious feats which he had performed at Balmoral. It was said the wizard's brass band was one of the finest to be heard.[16]

There was Billy Purvis the conjuror and clown who one year at Glasgow Fair with his establishment called the Victoria had a company of twenty performers and an orchestra of seven performing drama.[17] There were the circuses of Cooke's, Ord's, Hengler's, Pablo Fanque's and Franconi's; the menageries of Wombwell's, Hilton's, Batty's, Mander's and Edmond's etc., who brought all kinds of animals from all over the world to the people of Glasgow. There were Theatrical booths,[18] waxworks, giants and giantesses, dwarfs, fat women, fat children, fortune tellers, peepshows, dioramas and all types of stalls selling sweets, toys, lemonade and ballads, etc. One interesting performer at Glasgow Fair was Mons. Chabert the Fire King who entered inside an enclosed hot oven accompanied by several dishes of raw meat, on being released from his fiery den he produced the meat properly cooked. He also swallowed large doses of phosphorus and inhaled vapours of sulphuric acid, arsenic and other dangerous substances.[19] Malabar's performances would fit in with the shows at Glasgow Fair.

David Prince Miller's monument in the Glasgow Necropolis,
the sculptor was George Edwin Ewing.

Part of Glasgow Fair at the bottom of Saltmarket opposite the High Court
from *The Northern Looking Glass* Volume One, Number Four, 1825.

Malabar was better known however as a wandering entertainer and had his favourite spots in Glasgow. Some of these were at Jail Square (now called Jocelyn Square), St Enoch's Square, a piece of waste ground in New City Road, North Frederick Street, Carlton Place, Infirmary Square, Sauchiehall Street and a vacant piece of ground at Bridgeton Cross. He also liked to perform at cattle markets.

The first thing he would do was to attract a crowd and then he would say, *"Now ladies and gentlemen, just be kind enough to make a circle, and I shall have the honour of performing before you this morning."* Now making a circle was the most troublesome part of the whole business. As fast as he made the impatient crowd stand back on the one side they pressed in on the other. To make matters worse the inner ring of admirers would be children keen to see a free show as they had nothing to give and kept back the people who could give. Malabar had the reputation of being good natured towards children but they must have been the bane of his life.

The following is taken mainly from an article in the *Glasgow Evening News* in 1888 which gives a good insight into the way Malabar could coax an audience to hand over their money, as well as how he could get his own back on children to the amusement of the crowd. *"Just be kind enough to stand back a little ladies and gentlemen. I am about to begin; if you keep your places you will all see well enough. Give me a little encouragement, ladies and gentlemen; I've had the honour of performing before all crowned heads of Europe, George the Fourth, His Royal Highness Prince Albert, the Prince of Wales, and the nobility and gentry of England, Scotland and Ireland. A little encouragement, gentlemen; I am just going to begin."*

This spiel usually had the desired effect. Coppers jingled on the flagstones which he and his wife gathered up carefully, all the time telling his patrons he was just going to begin. A little more encouragement and he would show them some of the most wonderful feats they had ever seen.   When the copper shower ceased, he would start to open his bag and arrange his properties, swords, balls, rings and other paraphernalia of his craft.

He began with a simple act such as spinning a plate on top of a stick, tossing it up and catching it on the point, balancing it on his nose, and so on, concluding by calling for a little more encouragement, and he would show them something else.   *"You see this sword, ladies and gentlemen,"* producing a long thin rapier, with a massive hilt and glittering blade.   *"I will swallow this sword to the hilt without spoiling my digestion, a little more encouragement please."*   Another shower of coins followed this appeal and while Malabar and Ann his wife were busy picking up the coins and returning thanks profusely, the impatient children at the rear would break the formation driving each other pell mell into the arena, upsetting all the arrangements.   Malabar would make a few frantic efforts to restore order without success and then in disgust would gather up his belongings and make tracks for fresh fields and pastures new.   The ladies and gentlemen enjoyed a hearty laugh at Malabar's discomfiture, but the children expressed their displeasure in loud and indignant protest.   When the juggler showed unmistakable symptoms of retreat, they raised a clamorous shout, *"that'll no do! Come on wi your show, Mall."*   Deaf to all persuasion, the old veteran struck camp and marched off the ground followed by his meek little wife carrying the paraphernalia on her back with the children trooping at their heels.

When he succeeded in gathering an attentive and appreciative audience around him he went through all his old feats, with a skill which was surprising for a man of his advanced years.   His devoted wife and constant companion took charge of the apparatus, and during the performance arranged the articles and handed them to him in proper order.   Each separate act however, required   *"a little more encouragement."*

"Now ladies and gentlemen, I have only got sixpence.   What I am going to show you is worth far more money than that.   Thank you, thank you.   Well, you are very good, that's tuppence, just please make up the shilling and I will have the honour of performing the sword swallowing feat".

"Look here now," again producing the weapon and flourishing it in the air.   *"There's no deception, ladies and gentlemen.   Examine the blade, real double tempered steel, sharp as a razor on both edges and warranted to cut two inches before the point.   How much have you got now?   One and tuppence.   Very good but it ought to be one and sixpence, I can't perform this feat under one and sixpence; just show us your generosity."*

To excite the audience he walked slowly round the circle, exhibiting the sword, drawing his fingers over the edge of the blade, and inviting anyone to do the same and satisfy themselves   *"that there was no deception."*   All this preliminary palaver kept the older portion of the audience in good humour, but the youngsters would interrupt him every now and then with an impatient,   *"What are you bletherin at, Mali?   Come on wi' your show."*

Occasionally he indulged in a little quiet humour to amuse the spectators and revenge himself of his young tormentors.   Having fairly exhausted the patience and drained the pockets of his patrons of stray coppers, he solemnly proceeded to business.   To see him swallow the sword was worthy of a penny any day.   Taking up position in the centre of the arena, he held the weapon aloft at arms length, and surveyed it with a serious expression.   *"You see there's no deception, ladies and gentlemen.   I will put the weapon down my throat."*   *"Tak' care an' no choke, Mali,"* some impertinent urchin shouts.   Heedless of the interruption, the veteran juggler inclines his head back till his eyes are looking straight into the sky, opens his mouth wide, and inserts the sword point between his lips.   Then, as if some sudden thought had struck him, he withdraws the weapon, and, resuming his natural position, calls out   *"Here, now, I want some of you boys to assist me with this feat; it's a very difficult feat to perform.   I'll give any of you a penny to come into the ring and help me to eat this sword."*

The offer of a penny generally drew out some greenhorn, who would step timidly forward to tender his services. *"Let me see if you will do, my man,"* says Malabar, taking of his bonnet and examining his head, and turning him round and round before the audience. After inquiring his name and age, and putting some other ludicrous questions, he tells the lad to stand still, and keep his hands by his side. The youngster begins to feel a little uncomfortable, but he is afraid to move. *"Now my man, are you going to swallow the sword, or will I do it?"* The boy looks amazed as he sees the awful weapon held up before him. *"Hold up your head, and open your mouth."* The boy obeys, and Malabar, seizing him by the hair of his head, draws the flat side of the blade across his throat. The poor lad yells "Murder!" when he feels the touch of the cold steel, and flies off in mortal terror, amidst the uproarious laughter of the audience.

This little pantomime concluded, Malabar again proceeds to business. Raising the sword in his right hand, he inserts the point in his mouth, shuts his eyes, and the process of swallowing commences. Slowly the blade descends and disappears in the cavernous mouth. With his left hand he presses his bare throat as if to facilitate the descent of the indigestible intruder. Now it is passing his chest, and he rubs his breast with his hand, and would contort his frame as if he were undergoing excruciating internal agony. At last the blade disappears entirely, and nothing is seen but the long hilt protruding from his mouth. In this position he allows it to remain for a few seconds, turning himself round and round that the spectators may obtain a full view of the accomplished feat, and then he slowly withdraws the weapon and exhibits the blade all moist and dimmed after immersion. It seemed to sophisticated onlookers a rather disgusting performance, reminding them of the feeding processes of a boa constrictor.

The police never interfered with his performances on the streets or felt they were a nuisance or causing an obstruction, many of them knew Malabar from when they were children. It annoyed Malabar in earlier days when his performance attracted thieves; they would surround the ring and plunder his audience. This stopped the performance and the people soon dispersed.

This drawing is from *The Edinburgh Evening News* January 10th 1976.

The only photograph of Malabar without his cup strapped to his head
from the Mitchell Library in Glasgow.

One article tells how after securing the usual ring of people, he would open his large carpet bag and produce his "props," an old pack of cards, three pieces of wood shaped like a policeman's baton, and the greatest of all, a thick leather cup with straps attached, and a round wooden ball. Taking up two of the sticks, one in each hand, he would, with their aid, lift the third stick from the ground, set it twirling, throwing it up into the air, catching it again with the other sticks, and setting it twirling and spinning again. This performance went on until there were sufficient coppers thrown into the ring to justify carrying out his next trick.[20]

Another article describes one of Malabar's tricks called his "William Tell" act, where a boy in the audience was invited to stand with an apple on his brow and after a few feints and flourishes with a rapier (not a bow and arrow!), Old Malabar split the youngster's apple neatly in two. At odd times he juggled oranges, hats and umbrellas.[21]

Drawing of Malabar in the storeroom of People's Palace in Glasgow.

Articles written about Malabar often say he was comparatively temperate in his habits, rarely indulging in intoxicating liquors, taking nothing stronger than beer in his latter days. It was said nobody could make him drink whisky or more than two glasses of beer and the only time he did not keep to this was when he was performing at Phillip's Circus in Glasgow. He was sent to fetch a glass of beer for the governor from one of the tents as there used to be drinking tents then at the Fair. In the tent was Batty of Batty's Circus and Billy Purvis who persuaded him to indulge in drinking, not letting him go until he had taken punch with them. Being totally unused to such a tipple, it made him so unsteady that when he began his performance, as he had to do immediately afterwards, he missed catching the ball in the cup, and he had a black eye for a day or two. This he claimed was the only accident he ever had while performing.[22]

Malabar toured Scotland, England and Ireland attending fairs and racecourse meetings. He travelled with Swallow's circus in 1861 in company with Tom Sayers and Harry Broome, the famous pugilists. He was well known in Dundee, in his prime regularly attending the fairs which were held on the Meadows. One year when buildings began to be erected on the Meadows the shows were moved to an old quarry, which was not large enough to accommodate all the shows. When the quarry was completely full with the large number of shows turning up, performers and minor entertainments arriving late could find no room in the quarry and had to be accommodated on a separate piece of ground. Malabar was one of these late-comers and had to erect his small tent on this piece of waste ground. Business was terrible and although Malabar shouted himself hoarse nobody came to his show, the noise of the brass bands and general babble of people coming from the quarry drew the crowds straight into the quarry. Desperate for business Malabar, arrayed in his gaudy robes, preceded to the entrance of the quarry with a speaking trumpet and shouted, *"This way, this way,"* and gesticulated in a wild way to draw the attention of the people. *"This way, this way,"* he shouted and ran off towards his own establishment. This had the desired effect and a large crowd soon gathered around his tent. *"Now ladies and gentlemen,"* he said, addressing the crowd, *"I have no band of music or flaring pictures to attract you like those shows in the quarry, but I can give you as good an entertainment as you will get there. Some of you must know me. I am Malabar, the great Indian juggler, who has had the great honour of performing before George the Fourth, Queen Victoria, and the Emperor of Russia. Step in, and I promise you, you will not be disappointed, and the charge is only one halfpenny each."* In a few minutes the little tent was crowded. Malabar then entered the circle, telling the audience that he was not so young nor so active as he once was, but he would do his best to amuse them and if they appreciated his feats they could oblige by testifying the same by clapping their hands, and if he said or did anything amusing they should laugh and enjoy themselves.

As he proceeded with his programme he kept the audience in good humour, and they laughed and clapped their hands, and at the close they gave the veteran three hearty cheers. The people outside, hearing the laughter and the cheering, thought it must be a good show, and when the audience came out they rushed in and filled the place again. That day he did good business.[23] When he entertained the crowds in Edinburgh, his favourite spot was Parliament Square.

Malabar was a humorist who could amuse his audiences with jokes and witty remarks. Throwing the heavy ball twenty feet into the air and catching it up in the cup strapped to his forehead was his great feat and it was generally reserved as the last item in the programme. At times when in a merry mood he would throw a potato up and catch it in the cup several times in succession, and concluded the exhibition by striking the potato as it descended on the edge of the cup, splitting it into two fragments. A feat which was received with loud shouts of laughter was when he threw a fair size potato high into the air and let it smash into pieces on his forehead.   He said this did not hurt as long as you used a soft raw potato that is pliable to the touch.[24]

Malabar's cup and balls in the storeroom of the People's Palace.
The cup is leather the balls are made of wood.

On display at the People's Palace in Glasgow Green for many years were these props of Malabar's performance, which includes his brass juggling balls and the ball he threw in the air along with the leather cup he fastened to his forehead to catch it in.   When the building was last renovated these items were removed to a storeroom and are now not on show.

Some of Malabar's props in the storeroom of People's Palace in Glasgow.
His three brass balls, his brass ring and one of the three sticks he juggled with.

It has been said that Malabar made his first appearance on the legitimate stage at Sadlers' Wells Theatre in London in a company with the famous Joe Grimaldi. He also appeared at Astley's Circus, various theatres in London and the Manchester Theatre Royal as well as at a couple of minor theatres in the provinces in his early years.[25] I have so far found no other evidence to corroborate this although it is said he was a familiar figure at all race meetings in principal towns and cities in Great Britain. We have been told how he appeared with young George Sanger at Hyde Park Fair in London; he also performed in Norfolk Street and Brown Street in Manchester.[26] He told people his wanderings had taken him from Penzance and every county in England to Aberdeen where he fulfilled a short engagement in the Union Hall. Malabar often related to many people on how he balanced his donkey before George IV at Ascot, by command of His Majesty.

It is believed Malabar's proudest moment was when he appeared at the Theatre Royal in Glasgow on April 23rd 1877, after being asked by Mr Glover the theatre manager to be part of the company in Dion Boucicault's[27] celebrated racing drama the "Flying Scud." Malabar was in his seventy-seventh year and he was employed to appear in the Derby scene doing his juggling act to make the scene more realistic. When the well known figure entered from the side wings, and walked majestically down to the footlights, the audience gave him a standing ovation. Malabar bowed his acknowledgements, and gravely and solemnly proceeded to give his performance, juggling with balls, rings and daggers, while showers of coppers rained on the stage from all parts of the house. When he had concluded his exhibition he had to take his hat round the other performers on the stage as a racecourse juggler would. On the second night of the performance most of the actors dropped real coins into the hat instead of the counters supplied for the purpose by Mr Wallace the stage manager, and Malabar to his surprise and delight, found himself eighteen pence richer at the end of his journey. He insisted, in spite of Mr Wallace's wrath, on making a second round, for the special purpose of thanking his friends who had patronized him out of their own pockets. It was a glorious triumph for Malabar on the Theatre Royal stage, and it was said to be one of the most successful events of the season at the Royal, but it was all too brief. The drama appeared for ten night's only.[28]

Illustration is from *Curious & Remarkable Characters* by Peter Mackenzie, 1891.

Poster of the *Flying Scud* when Malabar performed on stage.
Poster from the collection of Gordon Bruce.

© Gordon Bruce

This oil painting of Malabar which belonged to Gordon Bruce, was stolen from his house.

When he was 71 years old the weather beaten showman said in an interview that for the first time in his life he was recovering from a serious and lengthened illness which had set him back in the world. He said it was thanks to a professional friend better off than himself that he weathered the worst of it and was now able to work for a living again. He mentioned his two brothers were still alive and prosperous in Ireland.[29] When he was over eighty years old, he could be seen juggling on Rothesay Esplanade during the summer.[30]

It has been said that his fellow showman David Prince Miller took a warm interest in "Old Malabar" in his declining days, writing an interesting account of his life, which was published at Miller's own expense. The copies being presented to Malabar and sold by him for his own benefit. Unfortunately I have not been able to trace such an article.[31]

The following poem was printed in The Bailie on April 25th 1877.

"OLD MALABAR"

As far back as we can remember,
We knew you as "Old" Malabar;
You're as white now as hoary December,
And perhaps on a par with Old Parr.

What trials you've seen as you wended
Through life since the time you were young;
How your food on three balls has depended,
And your bed on a balance was hung.

How the knave took the king, still you tell us,
When you played before George and his train:
You're the prince of all mountebank fellows,
You conceited old juggler vain.

At fairs you're the welcomest comer,
All Britain by turns you have spanned;
At coast-towns, again, in the summer,
Your footprints you leave on the sand.

When you swallowed the sword (cold emetic!)
How fear paled our young faces o'er;
And you puzzled our green arithmetic,
In counting the "just tuppence more."

We have watched you, and often you've told us,
For sixpence strange feats would be shown-
In our lives you have many times sold us,
And you live now by selling your own.

That a donkey you held on your chin, now
The story we never allowed;
But come, you sly rogue, just give in now,
Was the donkey not picked from the crowd?

In all trades we discover the trickster;
On 'change, what are bears? What are bulls?
Just to instance your own little trick, sir-
'Tis the donkey to tickle the fools.

Life itself's but a trick- who'll gainsay it?
And Time the arch wizard to plan;
His "Hi! Presto! Change! All obey it-
Old Death is the property man.

Photograph of Malabar in the storeroom of the People's Palace in Glasgow.

It must have been a sad day on 29th January 1883 when Malabar applied to the Glasgow Poor Law for relief. Application for relief number 57958 tells of the inspectors visit at 10 a.m. on 30th January 1883 to Patrick Feenie (sic) at 9 McPherson Street, one floor up. It states he is a widower age 82 whose wife Ann Ransom died ten years before in Stockton on Tees and they had no family. His occupation was given as a showman well known as Old Malabar and his disability was given as paralysis, adding he seems very ill. It was his first and only application when he was admitted to the Poorhouse; he came out of the Poorhouse in 1st of June 1883.[32]

Malabar made an appearance at the ceremony of the laying of the foundation stone of Glasgow Municipal Buildings at George's Square on 6th October 1883. The aged juggler was brought forth arrayed in his professional attire and seated in a carriage as part of the procession. He was a conspicuous figure in the grand parade and he was recognised by thousands of the spectators. Although he tried to take an interest in the proceedings and surveyed the crowds that lined the thoroughfares along the route, he was weak and ill and could only smile faintly in answer to his name.[33]

On being asked late in life if he could make a lot of money in his line of work, Malabar said sometimes he only made two shillings a day but at other times he could make ten or more shillings.[34]

In the showman's newspaper *The Era* dated the 10th November 1883 there was the announcement of Old Malabar's death.

"There died on Tuesday morning, somewhat suddenly, in McPherson Street, in the central district of Glasgow, a character who had been well known for many years in this quarter and throughout the country under the name of "Old Malabar," and who claimed to be the oldest showman in the world."

At the time of his death in his eighty-third year, his death took place in the house of Hugh Archer, with whom he lodged at 9, McPherson Street. He was out performing on Monday apparently in his usual health. On Tuesday morning he asked Mrs Archer to bring him some provisions, and when his landlady returned with these she found him dead.[35]

His wife, his constant companion for forty years, had died about ten years earlier, and Old Malabar was left alone, to struggle on against adversity and failing strength. With a brave, independent spirit he toiled on, resolved to make his last crust, and be in harness rather than go back to the Poorhouse.[36]

His death certificate showed it was Catherine Archer who reported Malabar's death. His profession was recorded as a Strolling Juggler. He died on the 6th November 1883 at 11.15 am aged 83 years; it was a sudden death and the cause was put down as old age, although there was no medical attendant to certify this on his death certificate.

Some days after the old man died, a corpse was brought to the University dissecting room, and it was reported that the body was Malabar. Touched at the supposed sad fate of one who had so often amused them, the students instead of dissecting the body, raised sufficient money among themselves to have him decently buried. The remains were not of Malabar, but the *Glasgow Weekly News* of 27th October 1888 thought the feeling of affection shown by the students towards the old juggler deserved to be recorded.

In the booklet '*Juggling Through Four Reigns*,' J.B. Findlay tells how Mrs Fell, who was running a Waxwork show in Trongate at the time of his death, provided the money for his funeral expenses and saw to it that the old showman was decently buried at Dalbeth Cemetery in Glasgow.[37] The Archdiocese of Glasgow who looks after Dalbeth Cemetery confirmed to me that Patrick Feeney, well known as Old Malabar was buried there in Section 9, Central Division, and Lair 910 on 8th November 1883. Their records said the cause of death was liver disease. Unfortunately there is no stone to mark his grave.

1861-1965

Extract of an entry in a REGISTER of DEATHS

Registration of Births, Deaths and Marriages (Scotland) Act 1965

2446418 C

No	1 Name and surname, rank or profession and whether single, married or widowed	2 When and where died	3 Sex	4 Age	5 Name, surname, and rank or profession of father, Name and maiden surname of mother	6 Cause of death, duration of disease, and medical attendant by whom certified	7 Signature and qualification of informant, and residence, if out of the house in which the death occurred	8 When and where registered and signature of registrar
757	Patrick Feeney Strolling Juggler (Widower Of	1883 November Sixth 11h 15m AM McPherson Street Glasgow	M	83 Years	———	Old Age Sudden No Medical Attendant	*(Signed)* Catherine Archer her X mark Inmate (Present) (Signed) James Hall Registrar Witness	1883 November 6th At Glasgow *(Signed)* James Hall *Registrar*

The above particulars are extracted from a Register of Deaths for the .... District ....
in the .... Burgh .... of .... Glasgow ....
this .... 1st .... day of .... February .... 2007 ....

The above particulars incorporate any subsequent corrections or amendments to the original entry made with the authority of the Registrar General.

Blackfriars

A.W. Brennal
.... Registrar
Glasgow District

Warning

It is an offence under section 53(3) of the Registration of Births, Deaths and Marriages (Scotland) Act 1965 for any person to pass as genuine any copy or reproduction of this extract which has not been made by a district registrar or assistant registrar and authenticated by his signature.

Any person who falsifies or forges any of the particulars on this extract or knowingly uses, gives or sends as genuine any false or forged extract is liable to prosecution under section 53(1) of the said Act.

Extract of Malabar's death certificate.

Malabar was a skilled performer and entertainer who obviously won the hearts of the people of Glasgow as shown by their actions after his death. Other performers tried to imitate his style and acts after he died but they were not as successful or respected as much by the Glaswegian people as he was. His memory has lived on in a way as illustrated below (and in the illustration on page 16) in later books and texts.

A modern Malabar? (c. 1930s)

"Penny-A-Yard" (1810-c.1875)

I feel that something should be said about this character that was once a familiar figure in the Saltmarket area of Glasgow, near Glasgow Green. The references are from the *Glasgow Scrapbook*, number two page seventy-one, in the Mitchell Library and in Sandy MacWhannell's *Rural Rambles Round Glasgow and Queer Scottish Folk.* Another interesting book with a chapter on "Penny-a-Yard" is Joe Fisher & Freddie Andersons' book *Auld Hawkie and other Glasgow Characters* with drawings by Dorothy Whitaker.

"Penny-a-Yard" made his living in the streets around the Saltmarket of Glasgow which had its characters including ballad singers, blind fiddlers and Malabar. Unlike Malabar, whom the Glasgow public were fond of, "Penny-a-Yard" was not popular, and was often arrested by the police for having a bad temper, a vicious tongue, and a huge capacity for drink. In person and manners he was more calculated to repel than to attract customers. Above average height, his figure was lank and drooping, while his walk was shambling and ungainly. His greasy, ill fitting garments picked up from various hand-me-down shops hung loosely on him; he looked more like a scarecrow than a human being. His face was haggard and debauched, while a fierce passion flashed from his darting eyes. "Penny-a-Yard's" real name was Edward Findlay or Finlay and it was said he came from Cork but he came from County Monaghan where he was born in 1810.

Day after day he plied his craft, shuffling along the outside of the pavement with a coil of wire around one arm, his fingers cramped into a peculiar shape around a pair of pliers with which he nimbly cut and manipulated the wire into links on his chain. The finished goods he strung around his neck. And always calling in gruff tones, *"Penny a yard; only a penny a yard"*, and that was how he became known as "Penny-a-Yard". A penny for 36 inches of chain was not an exorbitant price, and it was astonishing how he could earn a living at such an occupation. The chains met with a ready sale, housewives and small shopkeepers buying them up for hanging keys and scissors and other articles. Children often followed him and when they became too numerous or annoying he would pull a hideous face, yell like a wild man, and go into a war dance. Terror stricken, the children would fly off in different directions, while he would have a chuckle to himself and continue his occupation, calling *"Penny a yard; only a penny a yard,"* as if nothing had happened.

Not only did he make chains but he was an inventive genius too, and made wire puzzles which were said to be very clever, and equal to the famous "Exhibition Puzzle," which was sold extensively in Glasgow during the Great Exhibition of 1888. He manufactured these in his lodgings and sold them on the streets. Whenever he appeared with a new puzzle he was sure to draw a crowd around him. *"New puzzle- penny each,"* he cried, exhibiting the wire combination. *"You can't take this wire off that loop; but I'll show you how it's done, and then you can puzzle all your friends."* He bet anyone five to one that they would not solve the puzzle. When no one accepted, with a great flourish he proceeded to unravel the tangled links slowly, explaining every move as he proceeded. Everything is simple enough when he demonstrated it, and his customers thought they had found out the secret, but, though they had seen the trick explained, they generally forgot some part of the modus operandi, and were more puzzled than ever when they exhibited it to their friends.

"Penny-a-Yard" was great with puzzles and in addition to his wire puzzles he concocted and procured arithmetical puzzles. These he had printed on cards, and sold them on the streets. When he launched out in the arithmetical line he delivered an explanatory lecture and a demonstration on a board with a piece of chalk. On such occasions he drew large crowds around him, blocking the thoroughfare and affording ample scope for pickpockets, which he could not prevent. He was not in league with the pickpockets and as far as it is known he was never accused of any sort of dishonesty. The police held him responsible for the crowds, and while he was doing a fair trade and taking money fast the constable on the beat would appear on the scene, and with his authoritative *"Move on now"* scattered his customers in all directions.

This police interference aroused the brash side of his character. He had strong passions, and when inflamed with drink he became like an infuriated beast. His blood was seldom off boiling point, for almost all the money he earned was spent in public houses. He resented the police interference in his business affairs, cursing and swearing at, and abusing them while challenging them to fight. As the constables knew well the character of the man, he was often allowed to vent his temper with impunity, but at times when he overstepped the bounds of toleration he was arrested. In the hands of the police he raved and howled like a mad bull as he struggled and fought against his captors. In the course of time he became a notorious offender and disturber of the peace and was repeatedly locked up. In consequence of this the continuity of his business and public performances would be broken as he disappeared for a month or two at a time from his favourite haunts.

His application number 63121 for relief from the Glasgow Poor Law on 19th January 1858 was the third time he had applied for relief. On his application form, it states that the inspectors visited at 11.00 a.m. on the 20th July 1858, which Edward Finlay (or "Penny-a-Yard") lived at 4 Marshall Street (front low door) and he was born in Ireland, County Monaghan. Also it states that he was 48 years old, his occupation was wire maker, he was married to Susan Dickinson (who was 28 years old) and they had a daughter Elizabeth of 3 years and a son Joseph who was 8 months old. He had a disability (a lame hand) and was married before to Cecilia Owens who died 5 years previously. In addition it states in large print, **"He is a great pest"**.

He was back in the Poorhouse on 20th July 1858 and again on 4th July 1862 where the application form states he had disabled hands. On 26th April 1867 he was ordered to the Poorhouse but refused to go in and was supplied with an order for medical relief which satisfied him. On 13th December 1870 his wife Susan Dickinson Findlay and daughter Elizabeth (who sold newspapers) applied for relief as they were both ill with fever. "Penny-a-Yard" was by now in prison for six months for assault and since the date of their last application he had been in prison as often as he was out. Again "Penny-a-Yard" was back in the Poorhouse on 17th October 1873 and again on 8th February 1875 where it stated, **"This character is now on the decline"**. The last trace of him is when he left home to go back to the Poorhouse on 30th March 1875.

"Penny-a-Yard" had no rivals but latterly through his drinking and behaviour the people of Glasgow lost any respect they might have had for him. He died in the poorhouse and was buried in the Southern Necropolis in Glasgow.

Detail from the painting of "Penny-a-Yard" (see back cover).

Appendix

Old Malabar from Rural Rambles and Scottish Queer Folk

Sandy MacWhannell (pseudonym of John Knox Christie) wrote this in 1896 in the Scottish tongue of the time and it is recorded here as some people may like to compare it with the words of today.

Paisley Races have aye been held sin' ever I ha'e min' in the month o' August, an' mony a queer character has turned up at the Seestu bodies' annual gathering doon aboot Paterson's Mound.

"Heather Jock," "Hungry Jamie," the Deuck," an' ither worthies were frequenters o' the race-course as regularly as Lord Glasgow or the Duke o' Hamilton lang syne.

It was there I first set een on Patrick Feeney, better kent by the public as Old Malabar.

It's a score years or mair sin' then, an' aften I ha'e had a bit wird wi' the auld conjurer when he was wanderin' aboot the streets o' Glesca to fin' oot a suitable pitch to start his performance.

Old Malabar was rigged oot in a hauf Oriental style o' dress, an' a turban wi' a cup stuck in front o't to catch the ball or tatties he whiles threw high in the air, an' keppit them i' the cup ane after the ither when they cam' doon.

He was a native o' Sligo an' son o' a respectable fairmer, wha welcolmed him into the warl' on his arrival on 20th February, 1800.

When only some year or sae oot o' his teens he left the Green Isle an' sailed to Liverpool, whaur he got in tow wi' a Chinese conjurer, an' learned the jugglin' profession.

He sune started on his ain account as a professional conjurer, an' for aboot seventy years travelled ower a' pairts o' the United Kingdom, attendin' fairs, race-courses, markets, an' ony public gatherin' whaur he had an opportunity o' showin' his agility an' collectin' bawbees.

His tricks were no' by-or'nar' new, for naedoubt they were practised in China thousands o' years afore Twang, his Chinese teacher, brocht them ower the sea.

He cud whirl a basin on the en' o' a thin stick 'til ane was dizzy leuckin' at it. He cud balance a chair or a table on his nose an' walk roon the ring wi't, an' he aften made rings, balls, an' daggers spin roon' his heid in an amazin' mainner, forbye balancin' a donkey when he cud afford to keep ane wi' ae haun; an' a' his tricks an' feats were cleverly dune, wi' seldom a hitch in the performance.

Malabar was a big, strong fellow, an' wonderfully weel-liked by the public. Ye see, he was weel-behaved, sober, an' honest, wi' some respect for himsel', an' that made ithers respect him.

Aboot ten years since I was ae day passin' George Square when I saw Malabar, wi a crood roon' him, performin' at the corner o' North Frederick Street.

His wife was sittin' in the middle o' the ring' an' handin' up to him the rings, balls, sticks, an' ither articles he used when performin'.

After gaun through some o' his feats he ca'ed, as usual, for a collection afore gaun on wi' his tricks, but the money wasna appearin', an' his wife had an easy job to lift up the coppers.

The fac' is, naebody wad mak' a start by flingin' in the first bawbee or penny. Malabar made a strong appeal for some ane to begin the collection, an' oot o' sympathy wi' his wirds I put my haun' in my pooch an' flung a coin I got there right at Malabar's feet.

"Hillo, there!" he shouted, as he lifted the coin, "this has been thrown in in a mistake," holdin' up a hauf-croon that Kirsty had gien me to bring hame a box o' penny cigaurs frae a tobacconist's shop in Argyle Street for her wee shop on the South Side.

Dod, I held oot my haun', an' Malabar gied me back my hauf-croon, wi' the remark: "Sure, I knew it was done by mistake, an' I'll be glad to get a copper in place of it, for I'm an honest man, though only a street juggler."

Weel, I was real pleased wi' his honesty, an' aye after that Malabar kent my face, an' was aye willin' to ha'e a bit palaver.

He didna drink, an' leeved a quiet, dacent life alang wi' his wife, wha had travelled the kintra wi' him for mair than forty years.

For a wheen years afore he retired ahint the scenes for aye he keepit weel aboot Glesca, an' made a fair leevin' by performin' at a' pairts o' the city; whiles oot Sauchiehall Street, a wee bit up a side street, next at Cranstonhill, or oot Sandyford way, an' then awa east or wast, but aye in the neebourhood o'the city.

In his young days he cud balance a donkey on the en' o' a ladder, an' ha'e the ither en' o' the ladder restin' on his broo, or even his nose.

Whiles he had the donkey standin' on a table, an' lifted baith the donkey an' the table abune his heid wi' apparent ease.

He needed a lot o' strength as weel's practice to perform wi' the donkey or a big cairt wheel that he whiles used.

In his auld age he didna venture very great feats o' strength, but was wonderfully clever wi' the daggers, throwin' balls an' knives in the air, an' spinnin' the plate abune his heid.

I had a lang crack wi' him aboot nine years sin', when he was engaged to appear on the boards o' the Theatre Royal, in Cowcaddens.

I met him ae night oot Paisley Road way, an' his wife wasna lang deid at the time. He was leuckin' dowie, an' no like Malabar at a', so I stepped up to him an' asked hoo he was gettin' on an' sic like, an' then we adjourned to a decent hoose to hae a talk.

Old Malabar wad only tak' a gless o' beer, for he was by-or'nar temperate for a professional o' the kin', but we sat chattin' for a guid while, an' he was unco prood o' his engagement to appear at the theatre.

His name was in a' the bills, an' he had ane in his possession that he laid on the table, an' pointed oot wi' pride the bit whaur "Old Malabar, the famous juggler, who has performed before the Royal Family and the aristocracy, and also before George the Fourth at Ascot, by His Majesty's own command, is engaged to appear on the following ten nights at the Theatre Royal, in Boucicault's stirring drama, 'The Flying Scud.'"

"What pairt dae ye tak'?" says I, after readin' the bill. "Faith, the same ould part I have played before His Majesty George the Fourth," said Malabar; "and, sure, it's the part I play on the streets of Glasgow, and, av course, I'll put my best fut fornenst me when I am on the boards."

Malabar appeared in a race-course scene, whaur a' the usual conglomeration o' thimble-riggers, card-sharpers, wheels-o'-fortune folk, gipsies, an' ither orra characters are gathered.

He was seen, when the curtain was up at the Theatre Royal, standin' an' flingin' balls, rings, an' daggers aboot his heid like at a street corner, an' for ten nichts only was a member o' the company.

I speared if he cud mak' much in his profession, an' he telt me whiles twa shillin's was a' he wad draw in a day, but that ither days he got maybe ten or mair.

"Ye see, it's like this," he continued, "when I was in my best days an' going from town to town, I made a power o' money, an', faith, I cud spend it , too.   I would make a ten-pound note some weeks, and many a week I did nothing."

After this interview wi' the auld juggler, I saw him at his auld trade whiles at a street corner, an' it was seldom I got a wird wi' him.

In the en' o' 1888 I saw a wee paragraph in an evenin' paper sayin' Old Malabar was lyin ill, an' he died on the 6th November o' the same year.

He had been at his oot-door performances a week afore, an' as he was nearly ninety years o' age when he died, he was a remarkable body in mair than ae particular.

He worked to the last, an' had aye been independent o' charity a' his life, an' nae doubt cud ha'e laid past money had it no' been for his prodigal Hibernian disposition, that made him spen' his bawbees as freely an' quickly as he made them.

NOTES TO PAGES

Malabar (1800 – 1883)

The number and detail of endnotes never seem to please every reader. Some feel there are too many, and they get in the story's way. Others, particularly those doing related research, want more.

I personally feel the two items a book, especially a factual book like a biography requires, are endnotes and an index. I have many books in my library with bits of paper stuck in with notes where neither of the two items has been included.

(1) Most references including his death certificate state that his name was Feeney, however the Glasgow Weekly News article in 20th October 1888 states his family name as Finnie.

(2) MacWhannell, Sandy. (Pseudonym of John Knox Christie) in his book *Rural Rambles Round Glasgow and Queer Scottish Folk* calls this Chinese performer Twang, however most references use the name Tusang.

(3) Mackenzie, Peter. *Curious and Remarkable Glasgow Characters* dated 1891.

(4) *The Dark Side of Glasgow* dated 1871 from a book of newspaper cuttings from the *North British Daily Mail* in the Mitchell Library in Glasgow. In this article Malabar tells of his life and describes Glasgow Fair around 1820.

(5) *Evening Citizen* (Glasgow) 18th July 1931 gives the years 1822 or 1823 as Malabar's first appearance in Glasgow at the Glasgow Fair held in Glasgow Green.

The Era 10th November 1833 says his first appearance in Glasgow was when he was attached to Ducrow's Circus performing in Glasgow Green. As far as I am aware Ducrow's Circus was never in Glasgow Green. Whenever Ducrow appeared in Glasgow it was in a theatre (for example the Theatre Royal, Queen Street in 1828) so I do not believe it was Ducrow's Circus he appeared in around 1822/3.

The newspaper cutting in the Mitchell Library in *Glasgow Scrapbook* No.2 page 70 titled 'Old Malabar a Glasgow Street Performer' says he made his debut at Glasgow Fair in a large circus, the manager introducing him as Malabar, the young Indian juggler from the Court of Scringapatam. (There was a Celebrated Indian Juggler (from Seringapatam) who was performing in Mr. Young's Assembly Room, Coldstream in the Borders on 10th, January 1818 but when you read the illustration of the bill reproduced in "A Rich Cabinet of Magical Curiosities" by Edwin A. Dawes in *The Magic Circular*, April/May 1977 it doesn't appear to be Malabar. See also Sidney W. Clarke. *The Annals of Conjuring* dated 2001 page 395.) The newspaper article also states how Malabar for years was a regular visitor at times pitching a tent and performing on his own while at other times taking an engagement in some of the larger establishments at the fair.

(6) *The Glasgow Herald* July 12th 1924 and the Archdiocese of *Glasgow History of the Glasgow Fair.*

(7) *Sketches from Glasgow* by J. A. Hammerton published in 1893. The chapter titled "At the Shows a Reminiscence of Vinegar Hill". Also No.15, Vol. 11. (New Series) of *The Detective* July 16th, 1885 with the article by The "Tramp" titled "Among The Shows" At Vinegar Hill, and, *The Glasgow Eastern Standard* 25th, July 1936 titled "When Vinegar Hill Was At Its Zenith - Veteran Recalls Great Days Of Gallowgate "Fair" Ground."

(8) Sanger, 'Lord' George. *Seventy Years A Showman* gives Malabar's height as six feet four inches high.

(9) Wild, Samuel. *The Original, Complete and only Authentic Story of "Old Wild's...a nursery of strolling players and the celebrities who appeared there. Being the reminiscences of its chief and last proprietor, "Sam" Wild.* Edited by "Trim." (i.e. W. S. Megson). Reprinted from *The Halifax Courier.* 1888. (Reprinted in 1989 by The Society for Theatre Research. Page 19.

On page 18 he tells how his father gave private lessons in conjuring to Professor Anderson, the 'Wizard of the North' and David Prince Miller.

(10) Miller, David Prince. *The Life of a Showman (1849).* Pages 7 & 8.
Apart from his autobiography he was also the author of *The Young Men of Great Britain Conjuring Book*, *Magic Made Easy* and *The Wizard King's Book of Magic*.

(11) In the book *Extraordinary Exhibitions* by Ricky Jay (pages 90 and 91) there is a picture of a small poster of Signori Spelterini balancing on his teeth a real living Ass at the top of a ladder while holding a fifty six pound weight in each hand. The poster (or broadside) is dated about 1830.

(12) *The Dark Side of Glasgow* dated 1871 in a book of newspaper cuttings from the *British North Daily Mail* in the Mitchell Library in Glasgow.

(13) Thomas Frost on page 114 of his book *Circus Life and Circus Celebrities* 1876 when describing the principles of balance said, *"Whatever difficulty there was in the feat of balancing a ladder, to the top of which a small donkey was attached, as exhibited in my juvenile days by an itinerating performer, - whence the saying, 'Twopence more, and up goes the donkey' - was due entirely to the weight of the animal; because, if it was properly attached to the ladder, the centre of gravity would be in precisely the same situation as if the ladder alone had to be balanced."*

The trick of balancing a donkey tied to the top of a ladder was fact but many phrase books consider it to be fiction. Ebenezer Cobham Brewer in his 1898 book *Dictionary of Phrase and Fable* says, *"Two more, and up goes the donkey - An old cry at fairs, the showman having promised the credulous rustics that soon as enough pennies are collected his donkey will balance himself on top of the pole or ladder, as the case may be. Needless to say, it is always a matter of 'Two more pennies,' and the trick is never performed. The phrase is used of a braggart whose actions do not come up to his pretensions."*

This is repeated in Eric Partridge and Paul Beale's book *A Dictionary of Slang and Unconventional English* and John S. Farmer's book *A Dictionary of Slang and Colloquial English Slang and Its Analogues.*

Terry Pratchett in his books *Moving Pictures* (page 282) and *Reaper Man* (page 191) uses, *"Tuppence more and up goes the donkey"* as one of his Victorian sayings. In his monthly online newsletter he says, *"Tuppence more and up goes the donkey"*, *a favourite saying of Windle Poons, comes from the parties of strolling acrobats who'd carry their props on a donkey. They'd make a human pyramid and collectors would go around with the hat declaring that "tuppence more and up goes the donkey" as well. But the donkey never got elevated because, of course, the collectors always needed "tuppence more".*

(14) *Glasgow Weekly News* 27th October 1888.

(15) Miller, David Prince. *The Life of a Showman (1849).* Page 133.

(16) *The Glasgow Herald* July 12th 1850, *The Glasgow Examiner* for Saturday July 6th 1850 and a *Guide to Glasgow Fair* 1850 in the Mitchell Library, Glasgow.

The Glasgow Citizen of Saturday June 15th 1850 gave a list of the towns Professor J.H. Anderson would visit before arriving at Glasgow Fair giving the same conjuring exhibition he performed at Balmoral. These towns were: - **Kilsyth** Saturday June 15th, **Lennoxtown** of **Campsie** June 17th, **Milngavie** June 18th, **Dumbarton** June 19th, **Alexandria** June 20th, **Renfrew** June 21st, **Paisley** June 22nd, **Johnstone** June 24th, **Lochwinnoch** June 25th, **Beith** 26th, **Kilbirnie** June 27th, **Dalry** June 28th, **Kilwinning** June 29th, **Ardrossan** July 1st, **Saltcoats** July 2nd, and **Largs** on Wednesday July 3rd. He added a word of warning at the bottom of his advert cautioning against being misled by a close imitation of Mr Anderson's Bills by a person travelling through the country professing to give the Royal Balmoral Entertainment.

In *The Glasgow Examiner* for June 29th 1850 a change in the towns he would visit was announced in an advert stating on Monday July 1st he would now appear in **Irvine**, July 2nd in **Ardrossan**, July 3rd in **Largs** and on Thursday and Friday 4th and 5th July at **Greenock** for the Fair.

It also said a special steamer would sail from **Arran** to **Ardrossan** on the 2nd of July in time for the Wizard's performance and return in the evening. A special steamer would also sail from **Helensburgh**, **Dunoon** & **Rothsay** to **Largs** on 3rd July arriving again in time for the Wizard's performance again returning in the evening.

(17) *The Pepper Box* No.18 July 18th 1840. Joe Ging in his article titled "The Morn's the Fair": a bi-centennial tribute to Billy Purvis (1784-1853) in Vol. 1. No.3 June 1984 describes his theatre, a booth measuring ninety feet by thirty feet. *The Glasgow Herald* on 17th July informs us that Billy Purvis's Victoria establishment gave snatches of drama and singing where the price of the boxes was three-pence.

(18) *The Glasgow Herald* 14th July 1859 reports of one booth performance at Glasgow Fair in 1859 when Richard III was seen with his sword in his right hand and an umbrella in his left for the simple reason that the rain was penetrating the canvas roof.

The Pepper Box No. 18 July 18th. 1840. *The Glasgow Story* on David Prince Miller tells how his booth on Glasgow Green staged Shakespeare's Richard III up to twenty times in three hours, and in The Battle of Waterloo he played the entire French Army. David Prince Miller in his book *The Life of a Showman* (1849) tells us that many actors he knew who achieved fame and performed before Royalty in the Theatre Royal, Windsor Castle, started off performing before audiences of rustic bumpkins in booths at fairs.

(19) One of the best books on Mons. Chabert and Signora Josephine Girardelli is *Learned Pigs & Fireproof Women, A History of Unique, Eccentric & Amazing Entertainers* by Ricky Jay, dated 1987.

(20) *The Evening Citizen* February 9th 1935 in an article by William J. Firth.

(21) *The Glasgow Review* Number Four 1946-47 in an article by James Speirs.

(22) Mackenzie, Peter. *Curious and Remarkable Glasgow Characters* dated 1891. I believe he was not always like this and in his younger years he did drink a lot. In "Lord" George Sanger's book *Seventy Years a Showman* I have already told how when George Sanger was a boy at Hyde Park Fair, Malabar's donkey had been stolen and he took the donkey's place balanced at the top of the ladder, on the chin, forehead, shoulder and arm of the juggler. He goes on to say,

"But Malabar was given to drink, and business being brisk, and coin abundant, he one day indulged too freely in beer. I did not notice his condition till after my own little

performance, and I had started to ascend the balanced ladder. When I did perceive what had happened my nerves gave way just as I was clutching the sixteenth rung. Malabar lost his balance, and down I came, ladder and all, upon the heads of the spectators. The show was broken up for the night, and, in fact, altogether. Malabar drank enormously and did not show again while the fair lasted. Worst of all, I never got the pay I had bargained for, and all my labour, my little tricks, my patter outside, and the risk of my neck inside the booth went unrewarded."

I surmise by the time Malabar reached middle age and certainly in his latter years his drinking habits had changed dramatically to becoming almost teetotal. This is the only time I have come across of Malabar having a booth.

(23) From a newspaper cutting from *The Glasgow Scrapbook* No.2 in the Mitchell Library in Glasgow entitled "Old Malabar, A Glasgow Street Juggler".

(24) *The Dark Side of Glasgow* dated 1871 from a book of newspaper cuttings from the *North British Daily Mail* in the Mitchell Library in Glasgow.

John Turner in volume two of *Victorian Arena the performers* listed a gymnast and stilt performer called Rennef. Real name Fenner. His performance consisted of walking on high stilts, with a large ball which he threw high in the air and caught on the back of his neck. He then hurled a smaller ball to a greater height and caught it in a socket band upon his forehead, the ball invariably landing in the socket with a pronounced plop! When he appeared at the Peel Park Gala, Bradford, in 1876, he was then billed as 'King of the Cannon Ball'.

(25) *The Bailie* May 2nd 1877.

(26) The Manchester Literary Club publication *The Manchester Quarterly* Volume 20, 1901. William Dinsmore's chapter entitled Old Malabar, juggler and acrobat.

(27) The famous nineteenth century American stage spirit mediums the Davenport Brothers first performance in London on September 28th 1864 was at the home of Dion Boucicault, the actor-dramatist, before an audience of scientists and pressmen.

(28) The appearance at the Theatre Royal appears in most articles on Malabar. *The Bailie* for May 2nd 1877 is probably the best.

(29) *The Dark Side of Glasgow* dated 1871 from a book of newspaper cuttings from the *North British Daily Mail* in the Mitchell Library in Glasgow.

(30) *The Glasgow Story* (1830s – 1914 Culture and Leisure section).

(31) *The Era* 10th November 1883 and Boase, Frederick. *Modern English Biography Containing Many Thousand Concise Memoirs.* This is in six volumes. Look in Volume one column 1031 under Feeney, Patrick.

(32) The Glasgow Poor Law on the database in the archives in the Mitchell Library in Glasgow.

(33) Findlay, J. B. *Juggling Through Four Reigns* dated 1945. It says in this scarce booklet how - *A special Souvenir Programme was printed. An enterprising firm of photographers had an advertisement on the programme as follow : - "A WELL KNOWN YOUNG LADY IN FULL BALL COSTUME WILL BE PHOTOGRAPHED EN ROUTE & CARDS DITRIBUTED FREE" Then came the name of the firm. But the "young lady"- who was she? Why, none other than "Old Malabar." What he was paid for this piece of showmanship we will probably never discover, but great praise is due the old showman for* *his never say die spirit.* Having searched the file held in the Mitchell Library and looked at the Souvenir Programme I have not been able to find the advert. In the obituary in *The Era* dated 10th November 1883 it says that on the occasion of the laying of the foundation stone of the municipal building that "Old Malabar" displayed himself sitting in a chair on a photographer's wagon. Malabar obviously did appear in the procession, however whether dressed as a lady we cannot be sure.

(34) MacWhannell, Sandy. (Pseudonym of John Knox Christie) *Rural Rambles Round Glasgow and Queer Scottish Folk* dated 1896.

(35) *The Glasgow Herald* on November 7th 1883 reports how on the morning Malabar died, he did not get up at his usual time, he stayed in bed, and there was no complaint of illness heard from him. At eleven o'clock he asked his landlady to get a cup of tea, she did so and placed it down by his bedside, but the old entertainer had expired without taking a single sip.

(36) A number of articles for example *The Glasgow Scrapbook* No. 2 tell how the citizens of Glasgow did not desert him in his hour of need. A subscription was started, and a fund was raised for the benefit of Old Malabar. The money was placed in the hands of a responsible committee, and a regular weekly allowance was paid to him as long as he lived.

(37) Page 112 & 113 in Judith Bowers book *Stan Laurel and Other Stars of the Panopticon, the Story of the Britannia Music Hall* tells of a tour through Pickard's Museum as reported in the July 1935 *Evening Times*. On the first floor was the Waxworks with members of the Royal families including Queen Victoria, George V, and Queen Mary etc. There was Napoleon Bonaparte and Lord Kitchener along with other leading statesmen and standing alongside was a waxwork of Old Malabar.

Albert Ernest Pickard arrived in Glasgow in 1904 and bought Fell's Waxworks. I presume when Mrs Fell arranged for Malabar's funeral she had a death mask made along with Malabar's waxwork which A. E. Pickard acquired when he bought Fell's Waxworks. James B. Findlay's booklet *Juggling Through Four Reigns* about Old Malabar notes that he bought the death mask of Malabar when A. E Pickard auctioned his Trongate Waxworks relics.

BIBLIOGRAPHY

Books & booklets

AIRD, ANDREW.
Glimpses of Old Glasgow. Aird & Coghill, Glasgow, 1894.

ASSAEL, BRENDA.
The Circus and Victorian Society. University of Virginia Press, Charlottesville & London, 2005.

BOWERS, JUDITH.
Stan Laurel and Other Stars of The Panopticon, The Story of The Britannia Music Hall. Birlinn Limited, Edinburgh, 2007.

CAGE, R.A.(Editor)
The Working Class In Glasgow 1750 – 1914. Croom Helm Limited, Kent. 1987.

CLARKE, SIDNEY W.
The Annals of Conjuring. (Edited by Edwin A. Dawes, Todd Karr in association with Bob Read). The Miracle Factory, Seattle, 2001.

FINDLAY, JAMES BLACK.
Juggling Through Four Reigns. Mac's Mysteries, Glasgow 1945.

FROST, THOMAS.
Circus Life and Circus Celebrities, Tinsley Brothers, London, 1876.

HENDERSON, GEORGE.
Some Personal Recollections of School Days In The Calton Forty Years Ago. Harry Hobbs Limited, Glasgow, 1914.

JAY, RICKY.
Extraordinary Exhibitions. The Quantuck Lane Press, New York, 2005.
Learned Pigs & Fireproof Women. Robert Hale Ltd., London. 1987.
——.

JOHNSTONE, T.
Motherwell Memories. 1938.

MACKENZIE, PETER.
Curious and Remarkable Glasgow Characters. 1891.

MACWHANNELL, SANDY.
Rural Rambles Round Glasgow and Queer Scottish Folk. Alex. Malcolm & Co., Glasgow, 1896.

M'DOWALL, JOHN K.
The People's History of Glasgow. Hay Nisbet &Co., Limited, Glasgow, 1899.

MILLER, DAVID PRINCE.
The Life of a Showman; and the Managerial Struggles of David Prince Miller. Edward Avery, London, (c1853).

PRATCHETT, TERRY.
Moving Pictures. Corgi, London, 1991.
Reaper Man. Corgi, London, 1992.
——.

SANGER,"LORD" GEORGE.
Seventy Years a Showman. C. Arthur Pearson Ltd., London, 1908.

URIE, JOHN.
Glasgow and Paisley Eighty Years Ago. 1910.

WAUGH, EDWIN.
Besom Stories. John Heywood Ltd., Manchester & London, 1881.

WILD, SAMUEL.
The Original, Complete and only Authentic Story of "OLD Wild's" a Nursery of Strolling Players and the Celebrities who appeared there. Reprinted from the *Halifax Courier*. G. Vickers, London 1888.

Newspapers & Magazine Articles

The Bailie. 1877.

Daily Record. 1936.

The Dark Side Of Glasgow 1871.   Book of newspaper cuttings from **The North British Daily Mail** in the Mitchell Library.

Edinburgh Evening News. 1976.

The Era. 1883.

Evening Citizen. 1907.

Evening Citizen. 1935.

Glasgow Herald. 1883.

Glasgow Review. Number 4, 1946-47.

Glasgow Scrapbooks. Numbers 2, 9 and 13. The Mitchell Library, Glasgow.

Glasgow Weekly News. 1888.

The Magic Circular. April/May 1977.

The Manchester Quarterly. Volume 20, 1901.

The People's Journal. 1954.

The Pepper Box. Number 18, 1840.

The Sunday Express. 1943.

Young's Glasgow Scrapbook. Volume 1. The Mitchell Library, Glasgow.

Reference Works

ARNOTT, JAMES FULLARTON & ROBINSON, JOHN WILLIAM.
English Theatrical Literature 1559-1900 A Bibliography. incorporating **ROBERT W. LOW'S** *A Bibliographical Account of English Theatrical Literature* published in 1888. The Society for Theatrical Research, London, 1970.

BOASE, FREDERICK.
Modern English Biography Containing Many Thousand Concise Memoirs. 6 Volumes.

BREWER, EBENEZER COBHAM.
Brewer's Dictionary of Phrase & Fable. 1898.

FARMER, JOHN S.
A Dictionary of Slang and Colloquial English Slang and its Analogues.

FINDLAY, JAMES BLACK.
Ninth Collectors Annual, A Catalogue of Books on Conjuring and the Allied Arts in the J. B. Findlay Collection. D. W. Findlay, St.Albans, 1975.

PARTRIDGE, ERIC & BEALE, PAUL.
A Dictionary of Slang and Unconventional English. Routledge,1984.

SOKAN, ROBERT.
A Descriptive and Bibliographic Catalog of the Circus & Related Arts Collection at Illinois State University, Normal Illinois. The Scarlet Ibis Press, Illinois, 1976.

TOOLE STOTT, RAYMOND.
Circus and Allied Arts; A World Bibliography. 4 volumes. Harpur & Sons (Derby) Ltd., Derby, 1958-71.
——.
Circus and Allied Arts; A World Bibliography 1500-1982. Volume 5. Circus Friends Association of Great Britain with Aardvark Publishing, 1992.

TURNER, JOHN MARTIN.
Victorian Arena The Performers, A Dictionary of British Circus Biography. Volume 1 and 2. Lingdales Press, Formby, 1995-2000.
——.
Twentieth Century Circus People, A Dictionary of Circus Biography, Volume Four- 1901-1950. Lingdales Press, Formby 2003.

INDEX
(People & Places)

Page